STRAIGHT TALKING ABOUT DRUGS

Tobacco

Capital City Academy
Learning Centre
Doyle Gardens
London NW10 3ST

Tel: 0208 8388778

An Appleseed Editions book

First published in 2006 by Franklin Watts
338 Euston Road, London NW1 3BH

Franklin Watts Australia
Hachette Children's Books
Level 17/207 Kent St, Sydney, NSW 2000

© 2006 Appleseed Editions

Created by Appleseed Editions Ltd,
Well House, Friars Hill, Guestling,
East Sussex TN35 4ET

Designed by Guy Callaby
Edited by Pip Morgan
Artwork by Karen Donnelly
Picture research by Cathy Tatge

ISBN 0 7496 6758 3

Dewey Classification: 362.29' 6

A CIP catalogue for this book is available from
the British Library.

Photograph acknowledgements
Photographs by Alamy (K-PHOTOS, Iain Masterton, Gianni Muratore,
Photofusion Picture Library, Horner Sykes), Guy Callaby, Getty
Images (Bruce Ayres, Tim Boyle, BILL BRIDGES, RICHARD A.
BROOKS / AFP, Ron Chapple, John Chiasson, Peter Dokus, Sean
Gallup, Richard I'Anson, Ida P, Maxime Jourdan, Junko Kimura,
George Marks / Retrofile, Eric McNatt, MPI, Simon Miles / Allsport
UK / Allsport, Doug Plummer, Jan Pitman, Picture Post / Hulton
Archive, Andreas Rentz, Jon Riley, John Ross, JOEL SAGET / AFP,
KARIM SAHIB / AFP, Evan Skylar, David Harry Stewart, Stock
Montage, Justin Sullivan, Chung Sung-Jun, Charles Thatcher)

Printed in China

Contents

Smoking is one of the most common and deadliest habits in the world. You have probably seen thousands of cigarettes smoked in your lifetime, although perhaps not by your family. Although fewer people smoke today than in the past, one in every four adults still smokes – and there are parts of the world where smoking is increasing.

A lot to lose

In the following pages, you will learn how important it is to stay away from tobacco, and just how hard it is to stop if you do start smoking. Most people who become regular smokers started when they were young. This is the time to get the facts straight: smoking does no-one any good and it does a great deal of harm to your health. It also means giving up a lot in later life, such as the chance to excel in sports, extra spending money and even life itself. There is a lot to lose.

Lighting up in a bar or cafe is becoming less common as many countries ban smoking in public places.

Most smokers have a hard time explaining why they started – and why they continue. They know it is harmful and many even know someone who has died from a smoking-related illness, such as lung cancer or heart disease. But at the same time, these smokers carry on lighting up when they go out for a drink, take a break from work or when they hear worrying news. Some smokers even light up when they learn about the dangers of smoking – because they are worried.

An ugly habit

Whatever the reason people start smoking, the habit soon loses its attraction. Apart from the obvious health risks, smoking is an ugly, unpleasant habit. Most people would avoid a room that someone was filling with smelly smoke.

But imagine how you would feel if you were that smoker. Your behaviour offends many people around you, even some of your closest friends. Your clothes have a stale tobacco smell that seems impossible to get rid of. Your fingers and teeth become stained. Your mouth constantly has an unpleasant taste and you are afraid to give anyone a kiss because you know your mouth tastes like an ashtray.

> **❝ *I've been smoking now for 11 years and the other day I did some sums to see how much I had spent in that time. It would have been enough for a new car. I need a car, because I get too puffed out trying to walk anywhere 'cos of the smoking as well.* ❞**

Greg, 25 years old, from Cardiff, Wales.

Part of a display of cigarettes in a German shop.

Mexican migrant workers gather the harvest in Kentucky, one of the leading tobacco-producing states in the US.

When people smoke cigarettes, cigars and pipes, the smoke they inhale comes from the burning leaves of the tobacco plant. This plant is grown in many parts of the world, usually on large farms, though some small farms in Africa and southern Europe also grow it to sell.

Types of tobacco

After they are harvested, tobacco leaves are cured – they lose their green colour and are dried so they burn more easily. Tobacco is cured in the sun, indoors in the air at room temperature or by being heated. Each produces a different taste. Most tobacco for cigarettes and pipes is heat-cured over an open fire to produce a stronger, smokier taste. Cigars are produced from air-cured leaves that have a mild taste. People who chew tobacco use sun-cured leaves because of their sweet taste.

All types of tobacco are treated with chemicals to make them burn more evenly or to prevent the tobacco from drying out too much and crumbling. In cigarette factories, huge machines roll out the tobacco before wrapping each cigarette in paper. The manufacturers usually add filters, which absorb some of the chemicals from the smoke. Cigars are also produced by machines, which roll larger amounts of tobacco inside a tobacco leaf.

Damaging ingredients

The scientific name of the type of tobacco plant that is used for smoking is *Nicotiana tabacum*. Almost all the 70 other species of *Nicotiana* first grew in North and South America. You might have one of these tobacco species in your garden.

Nicotine is one of the many chemicals contained in the tobacco plant. It is the active ingredient of a cigarette and makes a smoker feel good for a little while, which is why most people smoke. But it also works on the brain, so smokers develop a habit. When they try stop (see pages 26–31), they have to fight the effects of the nicotine.

Many other chemicals in tobacco smoke blend together as the tobacco burns. They form a sticky, brownish substance called tar. It is tar that discolours the teeth and fingers of regular smokers. But tar does far more than cause stains. Although much of the tar leaves the body when the person breathes out smoke, some collects in the windpipe and lungs. Many of the worst diseases linked to smoking (see pages 22–25) are caused by the damage that tar does to the lungs.

Tobacco companies sell light cigarettes, which they advertise as being low in tar and nicotine. The companies say that light cigarettes are less harmful than full-strength cigarettes, but research shows that smokers simply light up more in a day to get their normal fix of nicotine.

Many Nicotiana *species have flowers which open at night and attract moths with their scent.*

Smoking-related gear (clockwise from top left): machine-made cigarettes, pipe, matches, rolling paper and loose tobacco for hand-rolled cigarettes, cigarette lighter.

How tobacco is used

Most tobacco users smoke cigarettes. They are sold in packets of 20 (or sometimes in packets of 10) and many smokers measure their habit by how many packets they smoke a day. The average smoker in the UK, Australia or North America smokes 18 cigarettes a day. Some chain smokers use up to three packs a day.

Before cigarette-rolling machines were invented, smokers rolled their own cigarettes using loose tobacco and individual papers. Some people still roll their own cigarettes.

Cigars and pipes are the two other main ways of smoking tobacco. It takes a lot longer to smoke a cigar or a pipeful of tobacco; in addition, cigars and pipes give off more (and thicker) smoke. For that reason cigars and pipes are less common in public places such as offices.

Tobacco can also be chewed, just as cowboys did in the days of the Wild West. This messy habit, which makes people spit out tobacco juice regularly, is rare outside rural parts of the US.

Taking snuff was common in the 19th century, but has almost died out. People would take a bit of tobacco powder between their thumb and index finger, put it to their nose and sniff it. They then needed to sneeze or blow their nose to get rid of the powder.

Staggering numbers

The scale of the world tobacco problem is enormous. The World Health Organization, a branch of the United Nations, estimates that a staggering 5.7 trillion (5,700,000,000,000) cigarettes are smoked every year. This means that people light up nearly 16 billion cigarettes every day, 650 million every hour, 11 million every minute and 183,000 every second around the world.

The tobacco companies that produce all these cigarettes – as well as 11 billion cigars and more than 2 million tonnes of pipe tobacco – make vast amounts of money and are powerful international businesses. Every person who gets hooked on smoking becomes a lifelong customer. However, there is a powerful alliance of anti-smoking organizations, international health groups, government health ministries and concerned individuals who are fighting the tobacco companies. This alliance spends large sums of money in its efforts to stop people smoking.

An Iraqi man who lost his leg in the US invasion of Baghdad leaves his young son to sell cigarettes by the side of the road.

Sitting Bull, seen here with a peace pipe called a calumet, was a Native American chief who led the Sioux people in their 19th-century struggle against the settlers.

The tobacco plant belongs to the same plant family as the potato and sweet pepper, which also came from the Americas. About 2,000 years ago, Native Americans chewed tobacco leaves to relieve toothache and swallowed them as medicine. Most importantly, they dried the leaves and smoked them.

Tobacco smoking became an important part of many Native American religions. Priests and other high-ranking men smoked tobacco at special ceremonies to ensure a good harvest, bring rain or provide victory in battles. Sharing a tobacco pipe with representatives of other nations – what we know as smoking the peace pipe – was a major part of Native American diplomacy.

> ** " Loathsome to the eye, hateful to the nose, harmful to the brain and dangerous to the lungs. "**

King James I of England and Scotland describing smoking in 1604.

The start of the tobacco industry

In the early 1490s, Christopher Columbus was the first man to take tobacco to Europe from North America. Frenchman Jean Nicot (after whom nicotine was named) introduced tobacco to France in 1556. By 1565, people had begun smoking tobacco in Portugal, Spain and England.

Englishman John Rolfe began growing tobacco in Virginia in 1612 and the colony soon became a leading producer of tobacco, along with the neighbouring Carolinas. The tobacco industry was built on slavery. Huge farms, or plantations, needed large numbers of people to plant and harvest the crop. Between 1619 and 1808 (when the US outlawed the transatlantic shipment of slaves), more than 600,000 Africans were sent to North America to work on tobacco and cotton plantations. Once in North America they were bought and sold like tools or cattle.

Europeans were hooked on smoking, chewing or sniffing tobacco, despite attempts by some people (including King James I of England) to stop the "filthy habit". People considered it stylish to smoke a pipe and having tobacco was a mark of a person's wealth as it was rare and expensive.

Some Europeans believed tobacco was good for their health. In 1571, a Spanish doctor called Nicolas Monardes wrote a book about the medicinal properties of American plants. He claimed that tobacco could cure 36 health problems, including headaches, toothache, swellings and open wounds.

FACT
The Maya people of Central America were the first to illustrate tobacco smoking. Some pottery created about 1,000 years ago shows a Maya man smoking tobacco leaves that were tied together with string. The Maya word for smoking was sik'ar, which is the root of our word cigar.

In 1492, Columbus sent sailors to the island of Cuba. They came back with tales of people who had flaming sticks (burning tobacco) in their mouths.

For many years, before the health risks became widely known, smoking was a normal activity. This 1950s photograph shows how many Americans liked to see themselves – the husband's pipe adds to the sense of comfort and contentment.

The modern industry

Until the middle of the 1800s, most tobacco was used for cigars, pipes, chewing or snuff. Then new strains of tobacco that burned more evenly were developed and the first machine to produce cigarettes was invented. Tobacco companies could sell millions of cigarettes, which were packaged easily and sent long distances.

By 1900, the number of cigarettes sold around the world had reached more than 3 billion, but this was only half the number of cigars. During the First World War pipes and cigars were hard to manage on the battlefield so soldiers from both sides smoked cigarettes. Governments included cigarettes in the soldiers' rations, with their food and drink.

More and more countries are banning smoking in public places, such as this underground station in Berlin, Germany.

The bubble bursts

Between 1910 and 1919, tobacco sales boomed; each year the number of cigarettes produced rose from 10 million to 60 million. A generation of young men had become regular customers and tobacco companies wanted to increase sales still further. Women were targeted with new, milder brands of cigarette.

Cigarette sales peaked in most countries during the 1940s. In Australia, for example, three out of four men (and one out of four women) were regular smokers in 1945. Then people started to learn about the health problems caused by smoking (see pages 22–25) from reports published by doctors.

The bubble of success and popularity began to burst. Tobacco companies tried to win the support of other doctors but, by the 1960s, they were forced by governments to add health warnings to their products.

The reaction against smoking continues to grow. The number of smokers has fallen dramatically in countries where smoking in public places is banned and tobacco sales and advertising are limited. Elsewhere, tobacco companies are trying to increase their profits and encourage new generations to start smoking.

"My friend Pete's dad runs a pub and Pete can get hold of cigarettes pretty easily. He shares them with me if I'm around, but we go to different schools now so I don't get free smokes so often. That means I have to buy them myself, if I'm in a different part of town, or get someone older to buy them for me if I'm closer to home where the shopkeepers all know how old I am."

Adam is 14 years old and lives near Reading. He smokes about eight cigarettes a day. Cancer Research UK reports that 450 British children take up smoking every day. Many will become regular smokers. Research has also shown that 95 per cent of regular smokers took up the habit when they were children. People rarely begin smoking when they are adults.

Young people sometimes smoke because it is risky or as an act of rebellion against the rules of their parents.

Hooked early

Why do young people like Adam begin smoking, especially when it is hard to buy cigarettes and when they know about the risks to their health? Some start smoking out of curiosity or as an experiment: they find some cigarettes and smoke them secretly. They probably think they are being daring because of the bad publicity surrounding smoking.

Others believe smoking is cool and grown-up. We all see images of people smoking in TV programmes and in films, despite the limits on tobacco advertising (see pages 36–39). Some teenagers believe smoking will impress other teenagers and mark them out as smart and adult. This need to impress people of a similar age is called peer pressure – it leads many young people to do dangerous or illegal things.

Finding it hard to stop

Experimenting and peer pressure are tied in with the way people become dependent on tobacco (see pages 28–31). So the answer to the question "Why do people smoke?" is simple – because regular smokers find it hard to stop. Government research has shown that seven out of ten adult smokers want to stop.

Younger smokers run the risk of becoming adult smokers who can't stop. Once they outgrow the need to impress people of their own age, they might feel that a cigarette calms them down or makes them feel happier. Bit by bit, as the habit becomes stronger, this need for a cigarette is triggered more and more often – whenever they have a cup of coffee or a break from work or a drink in the pub when they are older.

People in stressful jobs sometimes use smoking as a support because they think it helps them feel a little more relaxed and on top of things.

SEARCHING QUESTION

It seems impossible to miss the clear message that cigarette smoking is harmful and even deadly. Yet more and more children begin smoking each day. Can you think of other reasons why they take up the habit?

Who lights up?

One in five of the world's population lights up regularly, despite efforts to control or outlaw smoking.

Governments and medical experts in Western countries, such as the UK, the US and Australia, have very detailed information about how many people smoke. They know how many more men than women smoke, how many teenagers are regular smokers and whether people from some ethnic groups are more or less likely to smoke.

This information helps with plans for anti-smoking campaigns. Knowing, for example, that most people who smoke regularly began as children means that many anti-smoking messages are aimed at young people. Knowing how a person's health improves once he or she stops smoking helps to support the advice that is used to persuade adults to stop.

The wider world

The number of people who smoke has fallen in countries with the most detailed information about smoking (and because of that, the most detailed anti-smoking campaigns and laws). However, smoking is increasing in China and other countries that spend less money on anti-smoking campaigns. Many of these countries have the fastest-growing populations, which means that even more people are likely to smoke in the future.

About 1.3 billion people (roughly one-fifth of the world's population) smoke cigarettes regularly. Despite the success of anti-smoking efforts in many countries, this figure is expected to rise. The UN Secretary-General Kofi Annan has predicted that an extra 400–500 million people will be smokers by 2050.

An elderly Cuban woman smokes a locally produced cigar. Cuba is famous for its cigars, and the country has depended on tobacco for centuries.

" Thinking about Chinese smoking statistics is like trying to think about the limits of space. "

Rothmans Tobacco company spokesman (1992), quoted on the World Health Organization Tobacco Atlas web page.

Men and women

In Western countries, more than a quarter of men and women smoke regularly. The rate is slightly higher for men overall, but more teenage girls than boys are regular smokers. This means that in 10 or 20 years' time, there could be more women smokers than men – unless the teenage girls stop.

The numbers vary greatly in other parts of the world. The World Health Organization has found that as many as 69 per cent of men in Indonesia smoke regularly, but only 6 per cent of men in Cambodia. The West African country of Guinea has the most women smokers (44 per cent) compared with less than 1 per cent in the Middle Eastern country of Oman.

In some cultures, women are not allowed to smoke, which explains the low number of women smokers in Oman, where about a quarter of men smoke regularly. For the same reason, only 2 per cent of Bangladeshi women in the UK smoke regularly (compared to 42 per cent of Bangladeshi men).

A woman stoops to stub out a cigarette outside an office. More teenage girls than boys are taking up the habit so female smokers could soon outnumber male smokers in many countries.

REGULAR SMOKING BY UK BOYS AND GIRLS (AGED 11–15), 1992–2004

	1992 %	1994 %	1996 %	1998 %	2000 %	2002 %	2004 %
BOYS							
England	9	10	11	9	9	9	7
Wales	10	8	12	10	10	8	9
Scotland	10	11	14	11	10	11	9
N. Ireland	–	–	–	–	8	–	–
GIRLS							
England	10	13	15	12	12	11	10
Wales	13	13	16	17	16	14	13
Scotland	13	13	14	13	16	16	16
N. Ireland	–	–	–	–	10	–	–

These figures are drawn from the British Heart Foundation's website. Until 1999, those for Scotland are for 12–15 year-olds; from 2000, they are for 13–15 year-olds. Those for Northern Ireland are only available for 2000, but in 1990, the figure was 12 per cent for boys and 13 per cent for girls.

Teenagers often begin smoking with their friends. The smoking habit can quickly take root, even if these young people find new non-smoking friends.

The young who smoke

The World Health Organization reveals that about half the people who begin smoking in their teens go on to smoke for 10–15 years. They become regular customers for the tobacco companies and high-risk adults for those trying to control tobacco-related illnesses.

Australian evidence shows that 13.8 per cent of teenagers are regular smokers – much less than the 24.3 per cent in 1984. Figures for the US and many countries in western Europe are similar. The position elsewhere in the world is alarming. The World Health Organization figures show that:

● **One in five young teenagers (13–15 years old) in the world is a smoker.**

● **Between 80,000 and 100,000 children begin smoking every day, and half of these are in Asia.**

● **About a quarter of young people in the Western Pacific Region (including China and Southeast Asia) will die from smoking.**

● **Teenagers around the world are influenced by tobacco advertising.**

SEARCHING QUESTION

Many teenagers smoke in remote places such as Greenland and the islands off the north coast of Australia. Do you think that they smoke because the health messages haven't reached them or might there be another reason?

This photograph is a real reminder of the link between smoking and money. Over the years, a smoker will spend large amounts of money to feed their tobacco habit.

Smoking kills millions of people around the world every year. In the UK, one in five deaths are related to smoking. It is the major cause of lung cancer and leads to a severe risk of a heart attack and other heart conditions. Smoking makes it harder for people to have children and can harm babies before they are born.

Smoking is the only cause of death – apart from HIV/AIDS – that is rising each year. In 1990, smoking was the cause of 3 million of the total of 30 million deaths around the world. That means that smoking caused 10 per cent of all deaths. The World Health Organization has studied smoking trends and predicts that in 2030, smoking will be the cause of 10 million of the 60 million deaths around the world.

EFFECTS OF SMOKING

Smoking tobacco has immediate and long-lasting effects on the body. Even smoking one cigarette will affect you. If you continue to smoke tobacco the effects become worse and create other, more serious problems. The lists below outline some of these changes.

Smoking a cigarette

● The chemical nicotine is absorbed through the lungs into the blood and then goes to the brain, making the smoker feel more relaxed and alert.

● The cigarette reduces the amount of oxygen in the blood and makes the smoker dizzy.

● The smoke irritates the nose and breathing passages. This creates mucus which, together with the irritation, makes the smoker cough.

After a year of regular smoking

● The brain craves more nicotine because it wants to reproduce the pleasurable feelings it has felt before.

● Smokers find it harder to breathe and often cough and wheeze. Exercising hard becomes more difficult.

● Lungs and breathing passages become irritated, increasing the risk of cancer.

● Smoking can reduce the growth of the lungs in younger smokers.

● Regular intake of carbon monoxide has reduced the blood supply of oxygen, which makes the heart work harder.

● Regular amounts of nicotine reduce the width of blood vessels, which slows the flow of blood.

FACT

About 12 times as many British people have died from smoking than from the Second World War.

Long-term effects

● The craving for nicotine (between cigarettes) is very strong, making it hard for a person to stop smoking.

● The risk of a smoker dying of lung cancer is at least 12 times higher than that of a non-smoker.

● Long-term smokers are between three and five times more likely to have a stroke than non-smokers.

● On average, long-term smokers have a 50 per cent chance of dying of a tobacco-related disease.

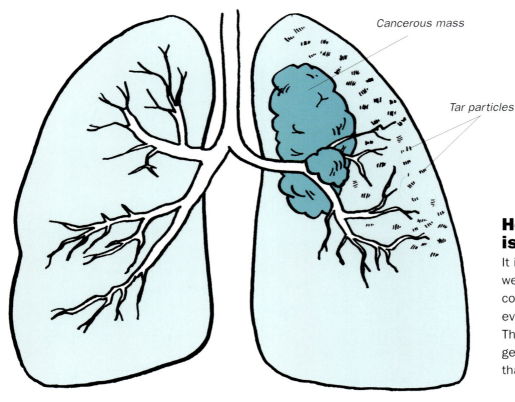
Cancerous mass

Tar particles

Tar particles left in the lungs by smoke contain chemicals that stop nearby cells from controlling their growth. They continue to grow and form a cancerous mass, which can spread throughout the body.

How the damage is done

It is natural to cough when we smoke, just as a person coughs after taking the first ever puff of a cigarette. This is the body's way of getting rid of tiny particles that irritate it.

Of the 4,000 chemicals contained in each cigarette, 400 are poisonous and 40 are known to cause cancer. For example, tobacco smoke contains ammonia (used in floor cleaners), acetone (used to strip paint), arsenic (used in ant poison) and vinyl chloride (used to make plastic).

Tar is the really harmful substance. Its chemical particles irritate the lining of the lungs and breathing passages and can trigger cancer. This serious disease, unless it is detected and eliminated early, spreads rapidly through the body. Cells become cancerous and the body becomes weaker and weaker as it tries – and fails – to stop the spread. Lung cancer is the deadliest risk of smoking. But even people who do not inhale smoke (for example, cigar and pipe smokers) run the risk of developing cancer of the mouth and throat.

Cigarette smoke also contains carbon monoxide, a gas that is found in car exhaust fumes. This replaces as much as 15 per cent of the oxygen that would normally be carried by the red blood cells. The body's organs, especially the heart, receive less and less oxygen. The heart is put under strain, forcing it to worker harder and harder. This extra work can cause the smoker to have a heart attack. If parts of the brain suffer from loss of oxygen, the smoker could have a stroke.

Smokers die younger

People have known about the serious health risks of smoking for more than 50 years. During that time, doctors have studied smokers and non-smokers to discover how bad the risks are. The evidence shows non-smokers live longer than smokers and heavy smokers run the greatest risk of dying young.

One of the most important studies was carried out by British doctors between 1951 and 1991. It showed that in middle age (which they defined as between the ages of 35 and 69), 41 per cent of regular smokers died, but only 20 per cent of non-smokers. Of those who smoked heavily (more than 25 cigarettes a day), exactly half died in middle age.

The May 2005 Rally Against Smoking in the US city of Chicago displayed 1,200 pairs of shoes – the number of Americans who die each year from tobacco-related illnesses.

SEARCHING QUESTION

Some people believe that smoking should be made illegal – and not simply controlled – because of the high cost of treating people who have smoked regularly. Do you think this is fair, or might it lead to other laws against junk food, which also has bad medical effects?

This woman in a British pub passively smokes the second-hand smoke from her friend's cigarette across the table.

People who have never lit a cigarette in their life can suffer serious health risks from smoking. The smoke from a burning cigarette combined with the smoke exhaled by a smoker can affect the health of a nearby non-smoker.

When smoke cannot escape from an enclosed area – or when several people are smoking – non-smokers can be deeply affected. Inhaling second-hand smoke is called passive smoking. Young people are at risk if their parents smoke in the sitting room of their home or in the car.

Everyone is at risk

Tobacco companies argue that the dangers of passive smoking are hard to prove. They say that anti-smoking campaigners have based their attacks on their dislike of smoking rather than on firm medical evidence. But the risks have been documented for nearly 20 years.

Passive smokers face most of the same medical dangers as smokers. BUPA, the UK's largest private medical insurance company, has calculated that non-smokers who live with regular smokers are 25 per cent more likely to develop lung cancer or heart disease than people who live in a smoke-free household.

The UK's Royal College of Physicians estimates that 17,000 children under the age of five go to hospital every year with illnesses caused by passive smoking.

"I come home each night with my clothes smelling of cigarette smoke. Sometimes my mum makes me hang my jacket outside if it's not raining." Eighteen-year-old Chloe is talking about her gap-year job working at a pub in Salisbury. Her clothes smell because of other people's smoke, but that inconvenience is less worrying than her health concerns.

"I don't smoke but I find myself coughing a lot more than before, plus my throat is sore a lot. Goodness knows what I'm breathing in – I know I'd never choose to work in an environment like this, but there aren't too many jobs out there that fit in with the time I've got free. The sooner the new laws (the UK laws limiting smoking in pubs and cafes) come in, the better. I was annoyed when I started, but now I'm scared."

Passive smoking is now an active issue in many parts of the world. Many countries and cities have banned smoking in public places and the workplace (see pages 36–39) in order to protect non-smokers and to prevent passive smoking.

SEARCHING QUESTION

Many smokers disagree with restrictions on where they can smoke. They believe that they know the risks when they light up, and that government controls limit their freedom. Do you believe they are right, or do you think this freedom means that other people have less freedom to breathe clean air?

You've probably met people who always seem to have a cigarette hanging from their lips. The ashtrays in their car and sitting room are always full of stubbed-out cigarettes. If you looked more closely, you might notice their fingers, teeth and even hair had a light-brown tobacco stain. These chain smokers are hooked on tobacco and it would be hard for them to do without cigarettes. Their lives seem to revolve around smoking and the need to have fresh supplies of cigarettes.

When we think of someone being hooked on a drug, we tend to imagine someone who needs a regular fix of heroin or a strong drink of alcohol. For these people, the drug has taken over their way of thinking and they can't imagine living without it – even if they know that it is harming them in some way. Smoking is another way of taking a drug – in this case, the drug nicotine. Just as people who become dependent on heroin or alcohol, people can become dependent on the nicotine in tobacco.

Some studies suggest that 90 per cent of regular smokers (most of whom would like to stop) began smoking when they were children.

20 minutes after stopping
Blood pressure and heart rate return to normal, leading to better circulation and more feeling in the hands and feet.

8 hours after stopping
Levels of nicotine and carbon monoxide in the blood are cut by half and the level of oxygen in the blood returns to normal. These changes reduce the chance of a heart attack.

24 hours after stopping
The body has eliminated all traces of carbon monoxide. The lungs begin to clear mucus and other materials that have built up from smoking.

2 to 12 weeks after stopping
The body's circulation has improved, making exercise much easier.

3 to 9 months after stopping
The lungs are working 10 per cent better than they were when the person smoked, helping to make breathing easier.

5 years after stopping
The risk of having a heart attack is about half that of a smoker's.

10 years after stopping
The risk of developing lung cancer is about half that of a smoker's. The risk of a heart attack is the same as that of a non-smoker.

Now for the good news

No one would argue that smoking is healthy, but some people believe that once they have started, there is no point in stopping because they have already damaged themselves. The truth is very different. Many of the risks linked to smoking can be greatly reduced – and often nearly eliminated – if someone stops. The success rate is even higher if young people stop before they have smoked for many years.

Doctors who specialize in smoking-related illnesses have studied how the body recovers from the damage done by smoking. The results are good news for those people who fear it is too late to stop. Some of the improvements take years, but the good news is that a smoker's health can begin improving within minutes of stopping. The panel on the left shows some of the health gains from stopping smoking.

An ashtray full of cigarette stubs is a reminder of the deadly nature of the smoking habit.

Smokers indulge their habit on the pavement outside Canary Wharf in London. Many companies around the world have banned smoking from their offices.

Dependence on nicotine

Doctors use the word dependence rather than addiction to describe the pull that a drug has on a user. Two types of dependence – physical and psychological – can develop and nicotine can cause both.

Physical dependence means the body suffers an unpleasant reaction when it stops receiving the drug. This is called withdrawal. It is the main reason a dependent person starts taking the drug again. Signs of nicotine withdrawal include feeling irritable and finding it hard to concentrate.

Nicotine creates a powerful psychological dependence for regular smokers. Like many drugs that affect people's moods, it tricks the brain into craving more. The result is that people link smoking with happy occasions or with their ability to cope with stress or unhappiness. The combination of physical and psychological dependence makes smoking one of the hardest habits to break (see pages 40–43).

A doctor performs a routine check on a patient's lungs. Most doctors advise patients to steer clear of smoking – or to stop if they already smoke.

SEARCHING QUESTION

Try to think of something that you might be dependent on – maybe sweets, fizzy drinks or computer games. What would you do if you had to give it up? Could you offer some advice to a smoker based on what you would do?

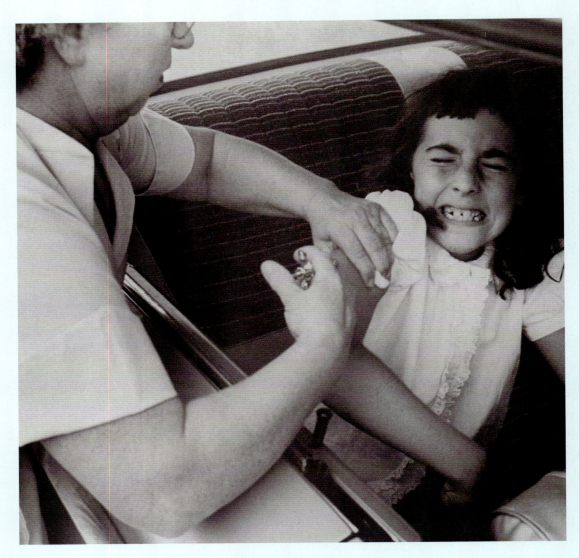

Health campaigns to inject children (sometimes painfully) helped control polio in the late 1950s.

Asimple question lies at the heart of the subject of tobacco and smoking: if we know it is so bad, why can't we simply ban it or take more steps to stop it? After all, scientists around the world helped defeat diseases such as smallpox and polio, and they are now battling against HIV/AIDS. Smoking, however, remains stubbornly with us.

There is no easy answer to the question, but it is worth looking at what makes smoking different from other killers. First, smoking is an activity, not a disease. Governments are unwilling to make activities illegal because they might be accused of restricting people's freedom. Second, some people – even non-smokers – think smoking has become too much a part of life to ban it completely. So the only way forward is to educate people to stop or, better still, not to start in the first place.

A way of life

For many years, especially before the health risks were well-known, smoking was part of everyday life. Film stars and sports personalities advertised cigarettes. Every sitting room and waiting room had ashtrays; people could smoke on underground trains, buses, planes and in the cinema.

Faced with such easygoing attitudes about smoking, and aware that a growing population meant more customers, tobacco companies became rich and powerful. They were an important part of a country's economy because they provided jobs (making, distributing and selling cigarettes and cigars). A large part of the cost of a packet of cigarettes went to governments in the form of tax.

It was never going to be easy to overturn this way of life. Once the dangers of smoking were publicized, governments had to warn people about smoking and teach young people about the health issues involved. Bit by bit, limits were imposed on the advertising and sale of tobacco (see pages 36–39), but governments faced – and still face — opposition from the tobacco industry and its supporters.

This British cigarette advertisement from the early 1950s concentrates on what seemed to worry people most about smoking – choosing the right taste and not getting bits of tobacco stuck on the teeth.

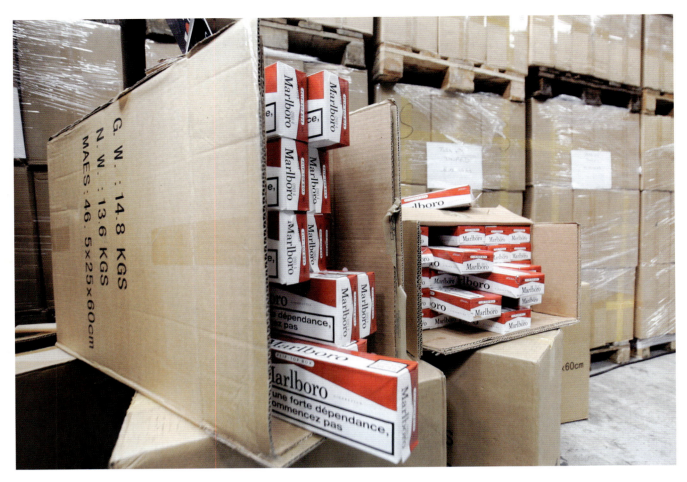

Heavy taxes on tobacco can lead to an illegal trade in imported cigarettes. These are some of the 1.8 million packs of cigarettes that French customs officials seized near Paris in April 2005.

The sin tax

The tobacco industry worldwide continues to thrive, despite attempts to prevent people from smoking. Part of the reason, as the companies argue, is that governments have come to depend on the tax money earned on the sale of tobacco. Such money is often called a sin tax because it is charged to people who are doing something wrong or dangerous. The price of alcoholic drinks also contains a similar large tax in many countries.

One example shows the complicated nature of the problem. The anti-smoking organization Kids Against Tobacco Smoke found that, in 1994, UK children (aged 11–15) smoked 1,154,000,000 cigarettes. The tax paid on these cigarettes, about 80 per cent of the total price, was £108 million. This amount was about 30 times more than the UK government spent in the same year on trying to reduce the number of children smoking.

The poor smoke more

Smoking costs an enormous amount of money, both for individuals and countries. The habit leads to daily expenses that mount up. In more developed countries, such as those in western Europe, North America and Australasia, people with money tend to smoke less than those who are poor. Poorer people are less able to afford cigarettes, yet many continue to smoke. It is a vicious circle – the habit makes them think that smoking helps them cope with their problems.

The same is true throughout the world. People in richer countries usually smoke less than those in developing (poorer) countries. The World Bank, an international organization that aims to help poorer countries develop, found out how much people spent on tobacco in several countries in the 1990s. In Bulgaria, families with at least one smoker spent more than 10 per cent of their household budget on tobacco products. In one district of China, households spent 17.1 per cent of their money on smoking.

Smokers in developing countries do not know the dangers of their habit because their governments lack the money to invest in large anti-smoking campaigns. So there is little information available and no health warnings on tobacco products. In addition, there are few – if any – controls on tobacco advertising (see pages 36–39). To make matters worse, tobacco companies offer good prices to the farmers in these countries for any tobacco they grow. They also help with fertilizers, pesticides and other farming needs. The result is that farmers plant fewer crops that could help feed the people in their country.

A cigarette billboard above a pavement in Kuala Lumpur, Malaysia. Such advertising often links cigarettes with an appealing view of the outside world.

During the last 50 years there have been many measures to limit the sale of tobacco, to make it harder to advertise tobacco products, to warn people about the risks of smoking and to make smoking illegal in some public places.

Doing the unthinkable

So far, only one country has taken the most dramatic step of banning tobacco products completely. On 17 December 2005, the tiny Asian kingdom of Bhutan in the Himalaya Mountains did what people had thought was unthinkable: it outlawed smoking in every public place and banned the sale of tobacco. Those who want an end to smoking might mark that date as a world holiday in years to come.

These young children from Bhutan will grow up in the first country to outlaw the sale and public smoking of tobacco.

Setting limits

Most regular smokers develop their habit when they are young, which means that young people are most likely to start smoking. Many countries, including Australia, the US, Canada and New Zealand, make it illegal to sell tobacco products to people under the age of 18. Other countries, including the UK, Ireland, Spain and Germany, set a lower limit of 16.

However, other countries have put no limits on how old a person must be to buy tobacco. For example, a nine-year-old can buy cigarettes in Greece, Portugal and Denmark. The same is true throughout most of the Third World.

Limiting or banning tobacco advertising is another way to deal with the problem. In 1971, the US banned all tobacco advertising on TV. More and more countries, including Australia, Italy, Finland, and the Netherlands, are banning all tobacco advertising. However, these advertising bans and limits tend to be mainly among the richer countries; cigarettes are still widely advertised in developing countries.

Formula 1 racing banned tobacco companies from advertising on cars in 2005 after many years of pressure from anti-smoking campaigners.

Health warnings

A very effective way to combat smoking is to target those most at risk – the smokers themselves. Many countries insist that health warnings appear on every tobacco product that goes on sale: cigarette and cigar packets as well as pouches of tobacco for pipes, cigarette rolling and chewing. The messages are clear and direct, telling smokers about the risks they take. There is no mistaking these messages, which by law must take up a large amount of both the front and back of the packets.

Since 2003, the health warnings in countries of the European Union must take up 30 per cent of the front of the packet. In the UK they include such general statements as:

● Smoking kills.

● Smoking can kill.

● Smoking seriously harms you and others around you.

Warnings on the back must take up 40 per cent of the area and are more specific:

● Your doctor or your pharmacist can help you stop smoking.

● Smokers die younger.

● Smoking can cause a slow and painful death.

● Stopping smoking reduces the risk of fatal heart and lung diseases.

● Protect children: don't make them breathe your smoke.

The latest Australian Health Authority warnings include a series of stark messages on the front of the pack and a scary image (linked to that message) on the back. Some of the most powerful messages include:

● Smoking causes emphysema (with pictures of a healthy lung and a lung affected by the disease).

● Smoking causes heart diseases (with an image of heart surgery).

● Smoking – a leading cause of death (with figures of annual deaths in Australia, showing smoking far ahead of motor vehicle accidents, illegal drugs and murder).

An anti-smoking advertisement in Beijing, China, makes a link between smoking and early death.

Banning tobacco

Many anti-smoking campaigners put pressure on their governments to ban smoking completely. It is a long and difficult process, but there have been some successes along the way. Issues of personal freedom and tax earnings from tobacco stand in the way of total bans, but the subject of passive smoking – and people's freedom not to breathe in smoke – has opened the door to partial bans in many places.

In 2003, the US states of California and Florida, along with cities such as New York and Boston, made it illegal to smoke in bars and restaurants. The governments of Ireland, New Zealand, Norway and Italy made such bans nationwide over the following two years. Scotland and Northern Ireland will introduce similar bans in 2006 and 2007, while England and Wales are deciding whether or not to ban smoking completely. Some pub and restaurant owners have argued that these bans will harm their businesses, but restaurants and bars in New York City reported an 8 per cent rise in business during the first year of their ban.

Smoking in pubs has been illegal in the Republic of Ireland since March 2004. Despite the ban, people still flock to the pubs for the drink, chat and music.

SEARCHING QUESTION
Have you read any of the health warnings that appear on tobacco packaging? If so, did you learn something that you didn't already know? What other messages could be added to warn young people against smoking?

Everyone agrees that smoking is one of the hardest habits to quit and that people need all the help they can get to cut down and eventually stub out their last cigarette. There are many classes, support groups and techniques to help people stop smoking for good. Many of the best anti-smoking organizations aim to help children or have special sections devoted to young people and their interests.

First steps to stopping

If you or one of your friends smokes, then you should think now about how to stop. The best place to start the process is in the home. Your parents should understand the pressure that young people face to smoke for they themselves also faced them. They, along with non-smoking friends and family members, can help you find your way back into a healthier way of life without tobacco.

Young people understand more about smoking if they can discuss it freely with their parents.

Schools and youth groups can help, too, by offering advice about stopping. The websites on pages 44–45 are great places to look for information and for stories about other people who have fought the battle against tobacco and won.

Nicotine gum and patches

Willpower and the support of others are not enough for some people. They need something to reduce the powerful cravings that make it hard to stop – and easy to continue – smoking. There are a numbers of products that can help. They usually contain nicotine, the drug that causes the cravings, but do not involve smoking. Two products are nicotine gum for chewing and nicotine patches which release steady amounts of nicotine into the body when attached to the skin of an arm. Of course, smokers who use these products will need to stop using them, too, but for some they are important first steps to a life without tobacco.

A Tokyo businessman smokes a cigarette in a SmoCar, which is a converted trailer where people can smoke freely. Although many Japanese people smoke, it is illegal to smoke on streets in parts of the country.

Educating people

In addition to providing information and advice about smoking, your school might be involved in anti-smoking activities at a local, national or even international level. These activities help build a sense of teamwork and support, and at the same time they are fun and might offer the chance to win some money for your school.

One scheme, known as Smokefree Class, began in Finland in 1989 and now has members from 21 European countries. It is aimed at 11–14 year-olds. Pupils enter as a class and pledge not to smoke for a six-month period. Classes that succeed enter a prize draw (for their school) and may win a special trip for the class.

Schools in Wales, the only UK schools so far to enter the competition, have been supported by Health Challenge Wales and by a range of popular figures, including sports stars Ryan Giggs and Colin Jackson, actor Matthew Rhys and pop star Linda Scott-Lee. By May 2005, 45 Welsh classes had won prizes ranging from £100 to £750.

In 2005 people in Seoul, South Korea, observed World No Tobacco Day by decorating the transport system with posters and artworks that linked smoking, illness and death.

INTERNATIONAL CO-OPERATION

The best way to spread the anti-smoking message around the world – and especially to poorer countries where smoking is on the increase – is to join an international effort. In 1987, the 192 member countries of the World Health Organization voted to do just that. They agreed to have a world No Tobacco Day on 31 May each year.

On No Tobacco Day experts and the public take part in discussions and other events to spread information about the dangers of smoking and the most successful ways to increase awareness and to help people stop. Each No Tobacco Day has a particular theme. Recent themes include:

- **2005**   Health professionals and tobacco
- **2004**   Tobacco and poverty, a vicious circle
- **2003**   Tobacco-free film, tobacco-free fashion
- **2002**   Tobacco-free sports
- **2001**   Second-hand smoke kills
- **2000**   Tobacco kills, don't be duped

Many activities and projects are imaginative and full of fun. For example, every baby born in Lithuania on 31 May 2005 received a T-shirt with the slogan "I am a born non-smoker". A special cricket match between health professionals and celebrities (including Bollywood stars) was held in Mumbai, India. Local rock bands in Sault Ste-Marie, Ontario (Canada) organized the Smashing Butts Breaking Down the Walls concert to send a message to the government to ban cigarette displays in local shops.

A Californian campaigner dressed as Ciggie Butts takes part in the 2005 Great American Smokeout, an annual nationwide event sponsored by the American Cancer Society.

SEARCHING QUESTION
Does your school take part in any anti-smoking activities or competitions? If not, can you think of any that would be popular with your fellow pupils? Could you set up a competition of your own?

Bollywood an unofficial term describing India's film industry, which is the largest in the world and based around Mumbai

cancer a dangerous growth in the human body that spreads by attacking neighbouring cells

cancerous describing cells that have been attacked by a cancer

cardiac concerning the heart

cash crop a crop grown for the money it will earn rather than to supply local people with the food they need

chain smoker a heavy smoker who seems to light up one cigarette as soon as the last one is finished

cured left to dry after harvesting

dependent having an almost uncontrollable need for something or to do something

diplomacy talking over and solving problems as a way of avoiding fighting or war

emphysema a disease which damages the tissues of the lungs

ethnic describing a large group of people who share a language, religion or other characteristics

European Union a group of 25 European countries that co-operate on a wide range of economic and political issues

fertilizer something added to soil to make it richer and better for growing crops

heart attack a sudden stoppage of blood entering the heart, causing great pain and sometimes leading to death

HIV/AIDS an abbreviation of human immunodeficiency virus, which can lead to the deadly condition Acquired Immune Deficiency Syndrome (AIDS)

loathsome causing people to feel sick or horrified

medicinal having health-giving qualities

mucus a substance produced by the body in response to an irritation or infection

national health a system in which the government uses taxpayers' money to provide health care for everyone

organ a part of the body, such as the eye or the heart, that does a specialized job

passive smoking breathing in the smoke from burning cigarettes and exhaled by smokers in an enclosed area

peer pressure persuasion from people of a similar age or social group to do something to remain part of the group

pesticide a chemical used by farmers to kill insects, mice and other animal pests that eat or damage crops

pharmacist another word for a chemist who supplies medicines

psychological to do with the mind

rations a daily supply of food given to soldiers

smallpox a potentially fatal viral disease that causes severe fever, pain and rash

snuff tobacco that is sniffed through the nostrils

species the most basic classification of plants and animals; two members of the same species can breed and reproduce

strain a member of the same species with slightly different colouring or other characteristics

stroke a blockage of blood in the brain which may leave someone unable to control movement, speech or even to think clearly. Severe strokes can kill people

tax money raised by a government from the people within a country

Third World a term to describe poorer, less developed countries mainly in Asia, Africa and South America

United Nations an international organization consisting of 192 member countries who meet to prevent war and to help each other overcome disease and other problems

withdrawal physical and psychological changes in a person who has stopped taking a substance after developing a dependence on it

Books

What's the Deal? J. Bingham (Heinemann, 2005)

Smoking S. Morgan (Hodder Wayland, 2001)

Smoking B. Sanders (Franklin Watts, 2003)

Choices for Teenagers: Smoking, Drinking, Taking Drugs and Experimenting with Sex N. Scott-Cameron (Corby: First and Best in Education Ltd)

Websites

Health.e.school Smoke Signals page (UK: Wales)
www.healtheschool.org.uk/primary/smoke_signals.htm
Wordsearches, songs and puzzles help to give primary-school children a clear picture about why it is cool not to smoke.

Kids Against Tobacco Smoke (UK)
www.roycastle.org/kats/
This eye-catching site is crammed with information, games, news and links about smoking.

Lungfish (New Zealand)
www.lungfish.co.nz/home
Competitons, personal stories, games and comics help make this one of the liveliest ant-smoking sites on the Web.

NHS (Smoking: UK)
www.givingupsmoking.co.uk
The Young People and Smoking section outlines the facts – and dispels the myths – about tobacco and smoking.

OxyGen (Australia)
www.oxygen.org.au/
A hard-hitting and lively site for young Australians about every aspect of smoking – and how young smokers can stop if they have developed the habit.

Quit and Win – Don't Start and Win (Europe)
www.quitandwin.net/
An anti-smoking competition organized by the European Network on Young People and Tobacco (ENYPAT) is the focus of a site packed with information and links about smoking and tobacco.

Smokefree Class (UK and Europe)
www.smokefreeclass.info
This site is aimed at children aged 11–14, the age when most people first experiment with smoking. It features a school-based competition, advice and links to tobacco sites around the world.

Index